A Prescription for Turning Tragedy into Triumph

A Prescription for Turning Tragedy into Triumph

∞

Dr. Irance' E. Reddix,
M.D. M Div, MTheo

Copyright © 2024 by Dr. Irance' E. Reddix, M.D. M Div, MTheo.

Library of Congress Control Number:		2024922646
ISBN:	Hardcover	979-8-3694-3295-2
	Softcover	979-8-3694-3294-5
	eBook	979-8-3694-3313-3

All rights reserved. No part of this book may be reproduced or transmitted in any form or by any means, electronic or mechanical, including photocopying, recording, or by any information storage and retrieval system, without permission in writing from the copyright owner.

Scripture quotations are taken from The Message Translation of the New Testament (TMNT), Copyright © 1993. The New Living Translation of the Holy Bible (NLT), and The Message Translation: The Wisdom Books (TMWB), Copyright © 1996.

Any people depicted in stock imagery provided by Getty Images are models, and such images are being used for illustrative purposes only.
Certain stock imagery © Getty Images.

Print information available on the last page.

Rev. date: 11/12/2024

To order additional copies of this book, contact:
Xlibris
844-714-8691
www.Xlibris.com
Orders@Xlibris.com
862561

Contents

From the Heart of the Doctor vii
Tragedy xi

T

Trials 2
Triumph 4
Taste 6
Temperance 8

R

Rejoice 12
Release 14
Relax 16
Renew 18

A

Awareness 22
Awakening 24
Alive 26
Achievement 28

G

Goals 32
Gifts 34

Greetings 36
Grace 38

E

Endurance 42
Energy 44
Empathy 46
Enthusiasm 48

D

Divine 52
Determination 54
Destiny 56
Deliverance 58

Y

Yes 62
Yesterday 64
Yearning 66
Youth 68

Conclusion 71

FROM THE HEART OF THE DOCTOR

THE WONDERFUL THING about life is that it is renewed daily. Plants grow; animals are born, mature, mate, and produce another generation; even bacteria and viruses reproduce to propagate their kind. We humans, however, are the only creatures God has made who have some control over our destiny. We have that wonderful thing called choice.

We can and do choose which direction our life can and will take. The even more remarkable thing about our lives is that once we give our lives to the one who created them in the first place, we are assured that our lives can be lived to the fullest and every bit of our potential is realized. We will not go to our graves with unmet promises.

I, as have most of you, have spent many years yearning to become more mature, yearning to be better at what I do, just yearning. Sometimes, my endeavors met with success. Other times, they only met with something else that had to be done. It was not in a flash of revelation or a divine inspiration that led me to the conclusion that drives my life now. An everyday, step-by-step process led me to this conclusion: life is a journey that can only be lived one experience at a time.

If I do not experience each one and learn the lessons each experience has to offer, then I will repeat it until I either get it right or die trying to get something that has been right at my fingertips the entire time. Once faced with this reality, my loving Creator steps in with this reassurance: "Throughout your entire journey, I will never leave you, I will never let you fall, I will always be here to instruct you. All you need to do is ask." This confidence floods my inner sense of inadequacy and now allows me to do all that God has purposed in God's heart for me to do.

Now is a new day
Possibilities are everywhere
Of course, possibilities are nothing until action takes place
They remain possibilities
Or better yet, impossibilities
Because the imps get in the way (Irance')

Inside the word *possibility* is the word *a-bility*
It takes ability to turn possibilities into actualities

TRAGEDY

TRAGEDY IS A word that most of us have become too familiar with lately. Water up to our chests, trees on our roofs, electricity that did not come on, spoiled meat, milk that had curds in it, a car that wouldn't start, a child that wouldn't leave home, a spouse that did. Either not enough money to rebuild our lives or enough money but nowhere to buy back the memories that were washed away in the storms of our lives. Tragedy can happen to us but doesn't dictate what happens inside us. We can allow our apparent tragedies to control us or strengthen us for life's long journey.

Tragedy

Every hour of every day, every day of every week, every week of every month, and every month of every year presents us with the possibility of experiencing tragedy. No one living is immune. Yet, our tragedies do not need to make us bitter and hardened. We should see our apparent tragedy as an opportunity to catapult ourselves out of our pit of despair and into the light of triumph. Allow these few words to be your daily prescription for turning your worst days into your best. Following is the word *tragedy* broken down into seven letters, each letter being given four different meanings, one for each day of the week, for every week of the month. Take each word and allow God to take you through your days of the week triumphantly, not tragically!

T

TRIALS

TRIALS ARE THINGS that come into our lives daily. They can be very small or enormous, depending upon our point of view. The trial can almost be too much to bear if we are standing underneath that mountain. If we are peering from the top, it can be so small as to seem insignificant. Whatever our perspective is, trials are only things that need to be overcome and gone through, not gone around. Remember that the size of the trial is directly related to our closeness to it. In other words, if we can pull ourselves away from the situation long enough to see the big picture, we can understand that the trial is only a small part of a bigger purpose.

Anyone who faces a testing challenge head-on and sticks it out is mighty fortunate. For such persons who are loyally in love with God, the reward is life and more life.

James 1:12 <s>(TMNT)</s>

Confession for This Day

I can do all things through Christ because He will give me the strength to do all (His) things, and He will not give me anything that I do not have the strength to do.

TRIUMPH

TRIUMPH MEANS TO overcome. This word is not used very much today except in sporting events, but it is a word that has been given to us as a birthright. We have been given the ability to overcome any and everything that is placed in front of us. Triumph does not come without the trial(s) first; otherwise, there is nothing to overcome, but is the victory sweet when we hang in there and fight. Triumph is usually associated with fanfare and celebration, so let us remember to celebrate every victory, large or small.

In the Messiah, in Christ, God leads us from place to place in one perpetual victory parade. Through us, he brings knowledge of Christ. Everywhere we go, people breathe in the exquisite fragrance.

2 Corinthians 2:14 ~~(TMNT)~~

Confession for This Day

There is nothing that can defeat me. There is no weapon that can, by any means, harm me as long as I am in the army of the Lord.

TASTE

TASTE IS ONE of the senses that gives life pleasure. Some of our most pleasant memories are of that great-tasting dessert or your favorite meal. Taste is directly connected to the centers of our brain that give us direct feedback. When something is pleasant, our brain tells us it is okay to experience that sensation again. However, experiences can leave a bitter and sweet taste in our lives. Although we may not be physically tasting anything, the bitter experiences can create a negative feedback loop inside Our brain, which produces churning thoughts and upset stomachs. It is up to us to rinse the bitterness away with the sweet savor of a good friendship, a well-loved movie, a quiet stroll, or just a moment of reflection on how wonderful it is to be able to take a moment of reflection. Taste and chew slowly the moments that make up every day. That way, we will not be so quick to miss the seasonings that make us mature.

Open your mouth and taste; open your eyes and see—how good God is. Blessed are you who run to him.

Psalm 34:8 ~~(TMNT)~~

Confession for This Day

From my mouth can come bitter or sweet things. I will ensure that I can stomach everything that comes out of my mouth if it were said to me.

TEMPERANCE

WHEN METAL IS taken out of the ground and undergoes all the processes that make it usable, we say it must be tempered. Tempering metal usually involves heating it to remove impurities or to melt other metals together to make it stronger. Whatever the methodology, it seems always to involve heat and pressure. It is not coincidental that God uses both heat and pressure to temper us and make us stronger. Temperance teaches us that no matter how high the temperature, there is always an end, usually in sight, and our resolve to remain is one thing that makes it all bearable.

But what happens when we live God's way? He brings gifts into our lives, much like fruit in an orchard—things like affection for others, exuberance about life, and serenity. We develop a willingness to stick with things, a sense of compassion, and a conviction that essential holiness permeates things and people. We find ourselves involved in loyal commitments, not needing to force our way in life, and able to marshal and direct our energies wisely.

Galatians 5:22-23 (~~TMNT~~)

Confession for This Day

Self-control means that I have learned to control myself and not others. I can be tempered (heated through God's testing and fire) because I have already gone through the fire and am not burned!

R

REJOICE

WHEN WE LOOK at the word *rejoice*, usually we think of an action, almost a command. But if you look at the word, one thing will become clear. Rejoice means to have re-joy.

> *[From the online etymology dictionary:* **rejoice:** *c.1300, "to enjoy the possession of," from O.Fr.[Old French] rejoiss-, stem of rejoissant, prp. of rejoir "gladden, rejoice," from re-, intensive prefix + joir "be glad," from L. gaudere "rejoice." The re- is meant to emphasize the verb, not to show repetition.]*

In other words, to bring again the joy that we once had. During these times, just take a minute to remember something that gave us great joy; try to remember how we felt during that time, the lift that was in our hearts, the feeling that, just for one moment, everything is okay with life. Now, take that feeling and apply it to today, no matter what has happened today. The feelings are very real, and so is the memory. In that way, we can rejoice and re-joy at all times.

Celebrate God all day, every day. I mean, revel in Him!
Philippians 4:4 ~~(TMNT)~~

Confession for This Day

I will not worry about anything I cannot change and will change everything I would have worried about. If I put my trust in God, His peace will guard my heart and mind.

RELEASE

JUST LET IT go. Things that have happened to us can often leave us wounded and hurting. At times, they are not even our fault or of our own choosing, yet frequently, we have made a significant contribution to the issue. Growth and healing come when we learn how to move on from the situation that has caused harm. As long as we hold onto it, it is as long as we are stuck in that situation. We can never get away until we let it go. Release the thoughts, intents, hurts, memories, and feelings that keep us stuck in the mud of our lives and watch the cleansing power of God heal our every wound.

The start of a quarrel is like a leak in a dam,
so stop it before it bursts.
Proverbs 17:14 (TMWB)

Confession for This Day

I will not allow anyone else's anger to infect the peace of my soul. I will release my innermost hurts and be filled by the peace of God that passes all understanding.

RELAX

TODAY, THIS WORD has been programmed into our day timer as "relaxation time." The real pity is that we usually see this time as wasted time, so we fill it in with other "important stuff." The fundamental importance of this word is that without relaxation, we cannot prepare ourselves for the battles ahead. We cannot inhale if we do not first exhale. We cannot wake up if we do not sleep first. We have yet to master the art of instantaneous transportation. It still takes time to go from one place to another. Let us make up our minds to let the taut muscles of our lives relax for a minute, breathe in the fresh air of the Holy Spirit, allow the washing of regeneration to cleanse us, and let the Son shine in our world. Take a quiet walk into the woods. Listen to your favorite music station. Sit down in your most comfortable chair and do nothing. Breathe in and out, listening to your breath sounds and feeling your chest expand and contract slowly.

Step out of the traffic! Take a long, loving look at me, your High God, above politics, above everything.

Psalm 46:10 (TMWB)

Confession for This Day

If it is for me, then it will be there when I get there. Since God has control over my life, then all things do work together for my good because I love the Lord and he has heard my prayers. I will relax and not be anxious about anything because God has my back!

RENEW

TO MAKE NEW again, to remind ourselves of something we have forgotten because we think it is old, used, tattered, or torn. The power of renewal is that the thing we need or are missing the most is likely already inside us. We just have to pick it up, dust it off, and take a new look at it. God has placed everything that is needed for greatness inside each of us. He gave each of us a unique purpose when placed in our mother's womb.

The purpose has sometimes been washed over, worried over, grown over, overcome, or, in other words, just forgotten. Take a space in your busy life and look over the things you have placed in your hopeless chest. Bring them back to God's light, let Him blow the dust away, and breathe new life into the purpose He has given you.

Don't become so well-adjusted to your culture that you fit into it without thinking. Instead, fix your attention on God. You'll be changed from the inside out. Readily recognize what he wants from you and quickly respond to it. Unlike the culture around you, which always drags you down to its level of immaturity, God brings the best out of you and develops a well-formed maturity in you.
Romans 12:2 <s>(TMNT)</s>

Confession for This Day

I have the mind of Christ. I can do all things because the mind of Christ within me gives me the strength and direction to do what He has purposed for me to accomplish this day. I can do all things through Christ; perpetual doing gives me strength to do even more.

A

AWARENESS

WHEN WE TRAVEL to any foreign country, the immigration officials always warn: "Be aware of your surroundings at all times…" It doesn't matter whether you are a foreigner in Europe, France, Africa, or the United States. We are all foreigners in another country. The more universal truth is that as children of the Most High God, we are all strangers (foreigners) and sojourners in a strange land.

This earthly realm is not our home. We are just to occupy it until He returns. We must always be aware that we are pilgrims, yet we are to rule this land that we occupy. Be aware that the rules and customs of this land are not always the rules and customs that God wants us to exhibit. In God's Kingdom, we are to love at all times, even when it's hard. In God's Kingdom, we are to welcome the ones who are strangers to us and give them hospitality. In God's Kingdom, we are to visit the sick and those in prison. In God's Kingdom, we are to clothe the naked and feed the hungry. We are not to be only renters of our heritage but full owners of the rights and privileges that Jesus has left us as joint heirs of the kingdom.

Think of yourselves the way Christ Jesus thought of himself. He had equal status with God but didn't think so much of himself that he had to cling to the advantages of that status no matter what. Not at all.

Philippians 2:5-6 ~~(TMNT)~~
Z-end

Confession for This Day

I am always aware of my surroundings. I know that I am surrounded by angels who bear me up in their hands lest I stumble and fall into temptation. I know that I am completely surrounded by Christ because my life is hidden with Christ in God. I know that I can and will surround myself with people who love God as much as I do and will edify me and not tear me down. I will do as God has commanded and love God's people.

AWAKENING

SOMETIMES, WE MISPLACE our trust in people, and because they are people, we get let down and disappointed. We are then said to have a "rude awakening" to the reality of the situation. With virtual reality, we can almost make anything "seem" to be idyllic. The actual meaning of *awakening* is "arousing, revival of senses, as in something asleep before."

Let us make every morning not just a "rude awakening" to the humdrum world we occupy daily. Realize that we have new mercies every morning and that this day has never existed before, so it cannot be just like yesterday. The people who let us down the day before cannot do it again because this is a new day, and we have a chance to be awake and not caught off guard by unmet expectations. Our expectations come only from the Lord, not from flesh and blood that perishes like the flower.

This is the day the LORD has made. We will rejoice and be glad in it.
Psalm 118:24 (NLT)

Confession for This Day

This is a new day I have never seen or experienced before. Upon awakening, I have a chance to make this the best day of my life so far since none of my expectations have been frustrated; I have put my trust in God. As long as I continue to do that, I am destined to awaken every day with a new promise, new hope, and new glories.

ALIVE

"ALIVE, ALIVE, ALIVE forevermore…" These are the words to a popular worship song. This song celebrates the presence and resurrection of Jesus who was slain but now is alive forevermore. One of the wonderful things about Jesus is that he is alive forevermore and came back and gave us that ability. We shall live and reign with him forever. Now, if that doesn't excite you because your life is not perfect, good news: Jesus gave us His life to live forever.

Jesus's life was fulfilled, free, and prosperous without spot, wrinkle, sin, or torment. The even more astounding news is that we can and do have the ability to have that life right here on Earth. We are dead to sin but alive to Christ, who lives, moves, and works in us and on our behalf. What a wonderful thing to have the life of Christ in us and be truly alive.

Indeed, I have been crucified with Christ. My ego is no longer central. It is no longer important that I appear righteous before you or have your good opinion, and I am no longer driven to impress God. Christ lives in me. The life you see me living is not "mine," but it is lived by faith in the Son of God, who loved me and gave himself for me. I am not going to go back on that.

Galatians 2:20 ~~(TMNT)~~

Z-end

Confession for This Day

Every time I take a breath, I am reminded that the Father gives me the very air that I breathe, and He has promised me the fullness of joy and the desires of my heart as I set my affections on Him. I know that my life is hidden with Christ in God.

ACHIEVEMENT

WHEN I WAS in high school, we had to take a series of achievement tests. These tests were supposed to assess how much I had learned in school and compare my level of achievement with that of other high school students around the country. These "tests" would then determine where or if you got into college, how much scholarship money might be available, or even if you were "college material."

Aren't you glad that God does not give us a standardized test of achievement and compare you to others like Abraham, Isaac, Paul, and John? God sees us as individuals and only tests the materials He has given us to master. Our achievements are not based on others but on how much we have dedicated ourselves to His service. When we dedicate our lives to his service, God gives us a crown of glory that can be worn daily.

> *By no means do I count myself an expert in all of this, but I've got my eye on the goal, where God is beckoning us onward—to Jesus. I'm off and running, and I'm not turning back.*
> Philippians 3:13-14 (~~TMNT~~)

Confession for This Day

I am an achiever. I can mount up on wings as an eagle and overcome every obstacle. The race that is set before me has been specifically designed for me by God, and I am destined to finish it and win.

G

GOALS

THE GAME IS tied. Your team has the ball, and there are only 20.6 seconds left on the clock. You are the star player, and your performance has been erratic all night long. It is up to you to win the game, but your confidence level is sagging. Do you call for the ball as the play has been designed, or do you pass it off to another player in hopes that they will be successful? Do you punt, pass, or kick in the game of life?

Are you the decision maker or the one who carries out someone else's decision? Goals are made to be attempted and then made. Goals sometimes are seemingly out of reach but can be accomplished with a little effort and practice. Go ahead. Take the shot. If you've got a good team (and Jesus is the best teammate anyone ever has), they will get the rebound and put the ball back into the basket for the winning score. And guess what? You will still get an assist, and in the end, we still win.

I've run hard right to the finish, believed all the way. All that's left now is the shouting—God's applause!

2 Timothy 4:7 ~~(TMNT)~~

Confession for This Day

I will run with patience this race that is set before me. I will never give up, nor will I give in. If I tire, I will lean on the everlasting arms of the Father who will never leave me or forsake me. I will obtain the crown at the end and reach my goal.

GIFTS

HAPPY BIRTHDAY TO you. Merry Christmas. Just because I was thinking about you. Almost any occasion is a cause for celebration and gifts. Gifts cause us to smile to feel warm and loved. Gifts can often say what words fail to express. What we might sometimes forget is that people are gifts too.

They have been put into our lives to enrich us, make us grow, complement our personalities, or sharpen our skills. They can be that missing part of us that we so dearly need to remain in balance. Take a minute to say thank you to that someone or those people in your life whom God has sent there to make your day. You might be surprised to find out that you have just given them a gift, and the only cost was kindness.

That is why the scriptures say:

When he ascended to the heights, he led a crowd of captives and gave gifts to his people. He is the one who gave these gifts to the church: the apostles, the prophets, the evangelists, and the pastors and teachers.

Ephesians 4:8, 11 (NLT)

Confession for This Day

I am a gift to the body of Christ. I am placed here for a purpose, and every day, I move forward to fulfill that purpose. I have also been given gifts from Christ, and I will cherish those gifts that are given to me.

GREETINGS

"WELCOME. YOU HAVE mail." This familiar greeting was heard thousands of times a day by those who are familiar with the Internet. And if you are not familiar with it, a popular movie made that phrase well known. It is a greeting by a mechanical voice that announces that someone has sent you something they want you to read. The greeting now may be a familiar "Ding" with the same meaning. What do the greetings that we use every day announce about us? Well, this isn't going to be a good day. What's wrong with you? Hey, what's up? Morning. (No good attached.) Praise the Lord.

Most of our greetings are just as mechanical as the voice or "Ding" on the computer. We have said them for so long that we have forgotten the real reason we even have a greeting: to make people feel welcome. If we start the morning off greeting the Lord, then just maybe the rest of our day will be spent making others feel as welcome as the Lord makes us feel. Good morning, Lord. I just want to say hello.

I will praise the LORD at all times. I will constantly speak his praises.
Psalm 34:1 (TLT)

Confession for This Day

May the words of my mouth and the meditations of my heart always be acceptable to you, Lord. I will keep my words sweet so that anyone whom I greet will only see and hear you, not my complaints.

GRACE

AN ANACRONYM OF grace can be God's riches at Christ's expense. How about an alternative? Growing richly and continuing (to) endure. Grace is that wonderful gift that God has given us even when we do not deserve it. Grace is given. It cannot be earned. It is like a little reward at the end of the day, even when the job is not fully completed, but the intentions of our heart are set to do so. It is the riches of God that Christ has released for us.

The best way to describe grace is via a brief story of a day in my life. I have been extremely busy over the past few months. I never seem to have enough hours in the day to accomplish all that needs to be done. One day, I looked out to the sky and whispered to no one in particular, "I just need one day that I can catch up with everything." Now, of course, one day is not enough, but it was a start, and looking at my schedule, there was not a free day in sight.

Two mornings later, I awoke to a phone call from a friend. "School has been canceled. Go look out your window." I had not even bothered to greet the morning; I had been so intent on my "routine." As I looked out the window, the ground was covered with snow, which is unusual during that time of the year in my part of the United States. I laughed with joy and breathed a quiet thank-you to the Lord who thought so much of me and my little prayer that he gave me a day to begin catching up. I am not saying that it snowed just for me, but grace teaches me that it is a gift.

You are the most handsome of all. Gracious words stream from your lips. God himself has blessed you forever.

Psalm 45:2 (NLT)

Confession for This Day

I am truly blessed. I have been given everything I need to complete the job before me. God's grace is sufficient for every need that I think I have.

E

ENDURANCE

STICK-TO-IT-IVENESS. THE ABILITY to hang in there whether others do. Endurance requires that we hold on past the point of comfort, beyond the boundaries of ease, well into the fields of strength. It takes stamina, intestinal fortitude, every long word you can think of, and more to describe endurance. The partner to that word is *patience*.

Without patience, none of us can endure. Remember that the next time you begin to complain about this race that God has set before you.

Do you see what this means—all these pioneers who blazed the way, all these veterans cheering us on? It means we'd better get on with it. Strip down, start running—and never quit! No extra spiritual fat, no parasitic sins. Keep your eyes on Jesus…
Hebrews 12:1 ~~(TMNT)~~

Confession for This Day

I am a world-class athlete in the race for the crown of life. I can and will endure everything that is set before me because nothing is too hard for God and God is living inside of me. I cannot lose because God cannot lose.

ENERGY

IN PHYSICS, A definition for *energy* is "the capacity for doing work." Work is force moved through distance. So, energy can be loosely defined as the capacity to move or exert force through a distance. Wow! Just think about it. The things we do every day, like walking, eating, going to work, and thinking, all require energy to do. That energy is our ability to move forces through distances. That means that we can say that mountain be removed and cast into the sea, and it has to move because we have energy to do so.

Now, I know that you will say that moving a mountain is different from driving a car, but remember, we have the mind of Christ. Jesus had the energy to walk on water, feed five thousand, heal the sick, and raise the dead. He promised us that we would do greater things than those because He went to the Father and left us with power from on high (the Holy Spirit). How many mountains have you moved lately?

And when the Holy Spirit comes on you, you will be able to be my witnesses in Jerusalem, all over Judea and Samaria, even to the ends of the world.

Acts 1:8 <s>(TMNT)</s>
Z-end

Confession for This Day

Conquering the mountains in my life is but a small thing. I must speak to them, know that they have been moved, and walk where they have just been.

EMPATHY

"IF YOU WERE just to walk a mile in my shoes," as the old saying goes. In fact, the saying says, "Before you start to judge me, step into my shoes and walk the life I'm living, and if you get as far as I am, just maybe you will see how strong I really AM." Sometimes, in our quest for perfection, maturity, and prosperity, we forget that, at some point, we all must start from somewhere. Our shoes have not always been as clean and shiny, our pants not always freshly laundered, our hair not newly coiffured. It is in our remembrance of where we are and where we are going. Do not forget the pain that God has delivered you from.

Do not forget the sorrow that He has removed from your heart. If you do, you might forget just how good He has been to you and begin to take His goodness for granted. Bear with and understand where your brother or sister is at present. Intercede on their behalf to God so that they may not have to endure what you endured to get to where you are. You did not like pain. Why do you think they do?

*Those of us who are strong and able in the faith
need to step in and lend a hand to those who falter
and not just do what is most convenient for us.*
                                    Romans 15:1 ~~(TMNT)~~

Confession for This Day

I am an anointed child of God who has brothers and sisters in the Lord. I will give the gift of my time, strength, or prayers to help sustain my siblings as they grow in grace. I know that as I give, it will be given to me good measure, pressed down, shaken together, and running over.

ENTHUSIASM

WOW! YEAH! HOORAY! Hallelujah! Enthusiasm can never be written without an exclamation point. That punctuation mark tells the reader that excitement is within the sentence. Sometimes, we are so busy reaching the next goal we can forget to celebrate the one that we just made. Our sense of adventure and wonder often becomes dulled by the everyday responsibilities of life and maturity.

Enthusiasm is that lost characteristic that allows us to be excited when we do not know the outcome of an event, not just look forward to it with dread. It allows us to praise during sorrow, rejoice in the middle of trouble, and sing when the melody should be the blues. More importantly, follow those events with excitement, no matter what the appearance, because all things do work together for the good of those who love the Lord.

Always be full of joy in the Lord. I say it again—rejoice!
Philippians 4:4 (NLT)

Confession for This Day

The joy of the Lord is my strength. I am excited to see what is going to happen today. I have strength, stamina, and expectation that something good is going to happen to me today, and I look forward to it with all my heart, soul, and mind.

D

DIVINE

HEAVENLY. WHEN THE word divine is mentioned, angels with white wings flying overhead and the sound of harps and heavenly choirs singing are the images that are usually brought to mind. Maybe we should expand our scope of the word to its real meaning: "the nature of God." God is loving but chastises His own. God is merciful and slow to anger but will pour out His wrath on the nations who do not obey His voice.

God is a supplier of all your needs yet requires you to take up your cross and follow Him. God is just yet gives gifts to whom He pleases. God is always in balance. He is the maker of all things and the creator of anything that was and is to come. Find the balance that is in God and pattern your nature around His definition of the divine.

Everything that goes into a life of pleasing God has been miraculously given to us by getting to know, personally and intimately, the One who invited us to God. The best invitation we ever received! We were also given absolutely terrific promises to pass on to you—your tickets to participation in the life of God after you turned your back on a world corrupted by lust.

2 Peter 1:3-4 (~~TMNT~~)

Confession for This Day

I am always in balance. I am not carried away by every wind of doctrine or opinion that comes along. I have made my stand, and it is on the Lord's side. I am not moved by what is a temporary condition, and everything is temporary except God.

DETERMINATION

THIS WORD, BY its very definition, includes the word *choice*. To determine anything, we must first choose that thing. The lingering question is, what have we chosen? Oftentimes, we set out on a path that may or may not be the correct one; however, because we have started, we are determined to finish it. Other times, we start down a path, realize that is not the correct path, leave in the middle, and start to accumulate a string of unfinished journeys. We are so determined not to make a mistake that we do not actually finish anything that we start.

Both are examples of determination; however, neither example is God's perfect plan for us. Maybe the best example of determination is the woman who is determined to get to the master healer so that she can be healed, the woman with the issue of blood. We could take one simple lesson from her: let us be determined to get to the author and finisher of our faith and let Him determine which direction to go from there. We will know if our direction is correct when it leads to the master healer and to peace

She was thinking to herself, "If I can just put a finger on his robe, I'll get well."
　　　　　　　　　Matthew 9:21 (T̶M̶N̶T̶)-end

Confession for This Day

I am willing to press toward the Master regardless of the intervening circumstances. I will make it to His feet and sit there until He has heard me and given me clear instructions on what to do. I know that He hears me because He loves me. I will wait upon the Lord.

DESTINY

When a swan is born, it may not immediately know exactly what it is. Its mother teaches it everything there is to know about being what it was born to be. Elephants take a tremendous amount of time with their offspring, teaching them trails and habits that will hopefully ensure that they live a long and prosperous life, for they have no natural enemies once they are grown. Monkeys even must teach their young progeny how to use tools to procure food. All have been destined to become what they were born to be.

We can teach a monkey how to do sign language, but his native language is still simian. We can get elephants to carry our loads, and even us, but their native environment is still the jungle. Swans look beautiful in our zoos, but they are captives. Destiny still reigns supreme over them, even if it is unfulfilled. There is a greatness born inside of each of us. God has put it there and fully expects us to fulfill it. It is not only the dreamers who aspire to greatness; they are just not held down by what they cannot see.

The fundamental fact of existence is that this trust in God, this faith, is the firm foundation under everything that makes life worth living. It's our handle on what we can't see. The act of faith distinguished our ancestors and set them above the crowd.

Hebrews 11:1 (TMNT)

Confession for This Day

I will achieve those things that I know within myself I can achieve with ease. Those things that I know within myself are a little bit difficult for me, but I will achieve them with just a little bit of work. Those things that I know within myself are impossible for me to achieve I will achieve with God's help through faith.

DELIVERANCE

What does it take to be freed from a situation? During slavery, the cost of a man's life was measured by the amount of work he could do and women by the number of offspring they could bear. In biblical times, a day's wages were valued at a penny.

How much would it cost to free you from your everyday toils, to buy your way out of ordinary to extraordinary? Would that deliver you from your worries, concerns, and fears? Good news. That price has already been paid. Better yet, you cannot repay what has been paid for you; you will just have to accept it as a free gift.

The LORD is my rock, my fortress, and my savior; my rock, in whom I find protection. He is my shield, the strength of my salvation, and my stronghold.

Psalm 18:2 (NLT)
ZZZZZ-end

Confession for This Day

I am delivered from all of my old destructive habits. I do not have to go back into something that no longer exists. The price that has been paid far exceeds the debt I owe, so I am free with change left over.

Y

YES

SUCH A SIMPLE word, a word that is one of the first ten words that children learn right after they learn the word *no*. Yes is so simple to say, yet it has gotten us into worlds of trouble at times or kept us from blessings at other times. Without this word, none of us would be employed. Without this word, no one would be married or divorced. Yes, can lead us to joy or pain. Yes, it is neither good nor bad. It truly depends on the contents of the yes.

Without this word, there would be no joy because there would be no affirmation of the positives that give us pleasure. There is only one yes that is imperative in your life, one yes that is the threshold between life and death. That is the yes to Jesus. Make sure that is the one yes that you say before you close your eyes.

It's the word of faith that welcomes God to go to work and set things right for us. This is the core of our preaching. Say the welcoming word to God—"Jesus is my Master"—embracing, body and soul, God's work of doing in us what he did in raising Jesus from the dead. That's it. You're not "doing" anything: you're simply calling out to God, trusting him to do it for you. That's salvation.

Romans 10:9 (TMNT

Confession for This Day

Yes, Lord, I am listening to you, and I hear you.

YESTERDAY

THE WORDS TO an old folk song stated, "Yesterday, all my troubles seem so far away." It is amazing that something that has never happened to us can and will.

We have 20/20 hindsight but can be miserably shortsighted when it comes to our future. Remember that yesterday is only fertile soil for today and fertilizer for tomorrow. It can only give us a perspective on what to expect but, in and of itself, has no predictive value. It cannot dictate what will happen to me. Today is a totally new day, and all things are possible. Allow your yesterday to lay a foundation for your future, not be a weight that chains you to your past.

But forget all that—it is nothing compared to what I am going to do. For I am about to do a brand-new thing. See I have already begun! Do you not see it?

Isaiah 43:18-19 (NLT)

Confession for This Day

My yesterdays are in the past, my todays are well underway, and my tomorrows are in God's hands. What do I have to worry about? I put my trust in the hands of the One who designed my future. How more secure can I be?

YEARNING

WHEN I WAS a young girl, I wanted a stuffed giraffe for Christmas. No particular reason; I just wanted a tall, stuffed giraffe. I had never seen one like I wanted and did not know anyone who had one. I got other stuffed animals, some even larger than the giraffe that I wanted, but I never got that giraffe. Now, as an adult, I have the ability to buy myself that giraffe, but the interest is not there anymore. At the time of my childhood, I had an intense yearning to have that giraffe. I planned what I would do with it, how I would play with it, and even where it would fit in my room.

Now that I can have it, I no longer even think about it. You see, we make adjustments in our life for disappointments and achievements yearnings may not always be realistic. They may not even be based on reality. They are things that we believe we want or need. Yearnings are not forever. They are a temporary displacement of affection. Let us learn to yearn for something that will never change or go away so that when that yearning is fulfilled, it will not become just a fond memory but a way of life. Let us yearn for the prince of peace so that peace may possess our souls.

> *As the deer pants for streams of water, so I long for you, O God.*
>
> Psalm 42:1 (NLT)
> ZZZZZ-end

Confession for This Day

Only you, God, can fill the thirsty depths of my soul. I yearn to be close to you and dwell in your secret place of protection. I release my inner most fears of detection and rejection and allow you to wash me clean and fill me with your love.

YOUTH

MY CHILDREN RUN from room to room in a never-ending game of hide-and-go-seek. There are only so many hiding places that a house can have, and I am sure that they have found them all over and over. Nevertheless, the game continues to hold hours of pleasure for them. Notice that I stated that the hiding places were all inside the house. The house represents security, safety, and, most of all, nearness to Mom. I am not going to tell you how often I have to say, "Keep it down to a dull roar. The neighbors three streets away might hear you." They laugh and continue their game with just a little less noise.

They are actively enjoying their youth. They do not worry about the light bill that must be paid to keep their game going; the furniture that was purchased, giving them a place to hide; the air conditioner/heater that keeps their environment comfortable; or the music that gives them the "cover" they need to sneak around. It is the same way in the kingdom. We should not worry about the price that was paid in blood to keep our life going; the things that furnish our lives and allow us to hide in our worlds, the wind of the Holy Spirit that keeps us under the protection of the Father, or the sweet intercession of Jesus to the Father that keeps us from being subdued by the enemy. Enjoy being an heir to the kingdom. You have everything that you need.

This resurrection life you received from God is not a timid, grave tending life. It's adventurously expectant, greeting God with a childlike "What's next, Papa?"

Romans 8:14-15

Confession for This Day

I am a child of the King. That makes me a princess or prince] I do enjoy every day and live it to the fullest. I can do all things because my Father the King has given me the power to always do His will, and if I do not know how to do His will, He left me with the King's ultimate teacher, the Holy Spirit.

CONCLUSION

TRAGEDIES CAN HAPPEN every day. There is loss, devastation, damage, and destruction. Yet the emotions attached to those things make them more of a tragedy. We feel anger, grief, Loss, uncertainty, Confusion, insecurity, and a host of other negative feelings. Personal and domestic tragedies are felt as keenly as national, environmental, and Worldwide tragedies. We can all feel that sense of gut-wrenching hopelessness in the face of tragedy. It seems as if our world will never be the same.

Yet, we serve a God who understands our feelings of hopelessness and despair. A God who knew at the beginning of time that we would need help to overcome situations; there would come a time when we all need to be rescued. Our God promises us that we are never far from his presence. He sees and knows our faults and failures and stands ready to support us. God is as close as the mention of God's name. What is the distance between our tragedy and our triumph? It is our perspective. In everything we do, everything that is done to us, and everything that happens in us, around us, and for us, God has a plan. God's plan is that we trust him, believe in him, and rely on him. When we can change our perspective from ohh God to O God.

The Adullum Alternative
Dr. Irance' E. Reddix, M.D.
3317 Kenjac RD
Windsor Mill MD 21244

Telephone: 318-348-5622

Email Address: irancereddixmccray@gmail.com